KATY LEWIS HOOD
&
MARIA SLEDMERE

infra·structure

BROKEN SLEEP BOOKS

Published 2020,
Broken Sleep Books:
Cornwall / Wales

brokensleepbooks.com

First Edition

Lay out your unrest.

Publisher/Editor: Aaron Kent
Editor: Charlie Baylis

Typeset in UK by Aaron Kent

Broken Sleep Books is committed to
a sustainable future for our planet,
and therefore uses print on
demand publication.

brokensleepbooks@gmail.com

ISBN: 978-1-913642-01-3

Contents

'that which binds us to the world in movement and keeps the world practically bound to itself'
Lauren Berlant

'the server is down, the bridge washes out, there is a power blackout'
Susan Leigh Star

'The wind whips the tight stems into a vibration,
But they don't break'
Margaret Tait

infra·structure

Katy Lewis Hood
&
Maria Sledmere

Transpiration

The way the wind feels, wonderful here
   the whir upon whir
Deciding a garden on remnant shingle
   a nuclear thought
Attains terminal currency

The burning has settled, there is a croft
   harnessing heat in smoke
This precarious light, its saucers of teal
   reply among dusk with letters
You talk of the radioactive skies of Cornwall

These document sunsets of endless orange
   is it enough, the criterion
Catches me out when I cannot, covet
   the prodigy pianist
Who rises from the night, collecting

Notes from airy wilderness lately
   toxic as song, she gasps
The latitude just exact, a vortex
   against those skirls beneath
Rising as islands, the ionisation

Stirs a permeable plane as sleep
   is flow in stark crescendos
Call it a starlicide, call it crush
   and the file size shrinks
Regardless of all these uranium colours

Things fall away. A travel hunger
   and the general solo
Arrives in micro, formerly known as
   the Anthropo catches
Inside a scene, the blueish diffraction

Is it all over me, in me
  a replicated face,
The sonnet astride a spiral jetty
  almost unnoticed, this gamma
Completion in droplets of crystal cloud

The narrative potential of all extinction
  to stick around, sybarite
With ambien balm as a blackout
  shotted for morning, porous;
Watching the sea transfer our future.

Th wa th wid fls, wdrful hr th whir up whir Dcidi a ard rmat
shil a uclar thuht Attais trmial currc Th buri has sttld, thr is a
crft harssi hat i smk This prcarius liht, its saucrs f tal rpl
am dusk with lttrs u talk f th radiactiv skis f Crwall Ths
dcumt susts f dlss ra is it uh, th critri Catchs m ut wh I cat,
cvt th prdi piaist Wh riss frm th iht, cllcti ts frm air wildrss
latl tic as s, sh asps Th latitud just act, a vrt aaist ths skirls
bath Risi as islads, th iisati Stirs a prmabl pla as slp is flw i
stark crscds Call it a starlicid, call it crush ad th fil siz shriks
Rardlss f all ths uraium clurs This fall awa. A travl hur ad th
ral sl Arrivs i micr, frmrl kw as th Athrp catchs Isid a sc, th
bluish diffracti Is it all vr m, i m a rplicatd fac, Th st astrid a
spiral jtt almst uticd, this amma Cmplti i drplts f crstal clud
Th arrativ pttial f all ticti t stick arud, sbarit With ambi balm
as a blackut shttd fr mri, prus; Watchi th sa trasfr ur futur.

Midnight Grid

super structural the lozenge enters a scalable blueprint throat of
electricity   enters   the thought   no system contends   capital
exactly broadened to enter for 12 hrs   offshore   <   > pace
designated   awareness   temporal gluttony   marking gear
comparable land wet & dry   the personnel know this   airlift forever
indebted company   working altitudes   develop excellence to blank it
foraging oil   another beautiful bike chain   <   professional interests
ultra depth   to authorise stones   > subsea   replicas
biggest   & nicest   rigs   need   our prissy grease
to contend   by type the cookie   cuts   us all in t i m e
disparaging magic   complete deep water   all of us sync better the beast
a fifth-gen ship   6 miles down in derrick   position   shut
down a hurricane   forget this   in 40 knot winds what happened w/o valve
the white noise   lulls you to sleep   in compliance   with
easy rainbows   molecular drip   positive   + honest attributes   dugout
black juice   guarantee affect   the treasury converts our workers   well

super
electricity
exactly
   designated

indebted
foraging   th
  ultra   biggest

temporal gluttony

i   n

          cuts   us all in t i m e
                   better
                       shut

disparaging

                         airlift forever

down
the white noise
easy

the treasury converts our workers

lowkey   subsea < nerve to new   working the clock   the million
dollar add   it on   additive kisses   the slick night clean   we like
white   strips   of lunar surplus   telling the blues > a while underneath
corporate   scrutiny kills   a salt distribution for legal reasons   these
luminous   coveralls keep us   sweet   some variants of energy
a cubic   standard on-duty switch   the disc place slips at noon   custodian
intake   facility implement   never a caging submersion   supply fail
feeding us   rice by moonlight permit   spilling terms of use   extend the platform

o

d t

us

lowkey
   add

    it on
  s   u r plus

luminous
cubic
intake
feeding us   moonlight

Yaw

    interior balancing   "just holding up"   centrifugal
  is a false force   hinging   the horizons moving
at night   point magnetic dispersals   some other time
  that could not be measured   in threes
    kilowatt hours   spoondrift broken from edges
  of waves   _ /_   for out of turn attention
voices rumbled / | jargonly   from either side
  of the hall   "we have more than we could use
    currently"   booming rhythms of maintenance
  parsed as armatures of care   propelling
bodies held   circling in the nacelle   inert only
  moments   even at breakpoint   for losses
    in torquing   interior   will not be curtailed

interior

of waves

parsed
bodies held

in torquing

a false force

not be measured
spoondrift

_/_
jargonly

booming
as armatures of care

moments
interior

"just holding up"
hinging

broken

"we have more"

in the nacelle

will

some other time

attention
either side
than we could use currently
of maintenance

for losses

Darkland

Ordinance rent

at basic scales

full ease with oil

all over the docks

oasis is better

to fill the throat

these railways sleep

telluric still

Investing a cloud

lightly of pesticide

in red-eye night

by uncanny fingers

to carry no scars

of noxious current

Unborn in Forth

attuned to our city

backwards the land

other works remain

prone to melt

locks itself

ordinance itself:
rent locks oasis land
is the better backwards
at melt basic to scales
prone to city fill our
~~the to~~ throat attuned
full remain ease works
with other oil
these Forth railways
in sleep unborn
all current over noxious
~~the of~~ docks telluric
night still red-eye
investing scars no a cloud
carry ~~by to~~ pesticide
uncanny of fingers
lightly

Divers

the basin a haw this a.m., sky eyedropped
               the contrails, made retrofit light. of burning:
bed nooked into wall and half the grey
               matter still awake when exhaust subsides

into elbow, old name for constants of shifting
               baselines overhead—hypnagogic tracks
in bitumen lines. dreamt sweeping membrane
               over debris, memory of pump installation

bedded in, built around, multiple units
               pass electric a blink. always the energetic
question going backwards and backwards
               until conservative by proxy, we sit on

our hands. looped converting work to heat,
               firmament nests matte. at a given height,
a bird's eye is taken as given as invitation
               for tenders, networked proximity or virtual

shaking, palm clamped too slow convexed
               over lens. the fruiting season: model
windfall of a plane would fly like a draining
               of fluid carbon fixing, evolutions ago

the basin   a.m.,   eyedropped

                                                            retrofit.

bedwall   grey

                                                awake when

elbow   for constants

                                                hypnagogic

in bitumen   membrane

                over debris   installation

bedded in   multiple units

                                    electric a blink

going backwards and backwards

                                                        by proxy

looped ~~converting~~ work to heat,

                                firmament ███ matte

invitation

                                        for tenders

shaking, palm convexed

                                over lens. the fruiting

windfall

                of fluid ~~carbon~~ fixing, evolutions ago

Brink

the folding of means for keeping working into pockets
of turf, skinned bluffs hedging tectonic and unclimbable.
the string for navigational memory is already cut
at all ends, though spun and ringed in paper, stapled
with the weight of something that might feed.

in one hand, whitewashed fibre; in one hand,
imperfect carapaces dense enough to shatter
diamonds scooped from streambeds, plasmic-
mapped. the telegraph wires image sinews laid out
the length of the earth, glutted wires' semaphorics.

imprinted in charcoal, the mineral linings of hills
repeat without solids, upturned ungrasp horizon
a paperless offshore. cloudcover: a wave through
dynamics of the undocumented, a plicature,
aligned with a plant. the minimum is knuckled

down undebted state-of-the- grazing on seawall,
white cliffs. woolled eyes run rings around light-
houses, alternating containers stack up slimmed-
down welfare garment. an apophany, a pipedream:
a selvedge of quartz that doesn't clock, beach, or rig.

imprinted
imprinted minimum
imprinted minimum quartz
imprinted minimum
imprinted

a length
a length of the
a length of the earth in hand
a length of the
a length

down undebted
down undebted nation
down undebted nation a selvedge
down undebted nation
down undebted

slimmed
slimmed garment
slimmed garment of a plicature
slimmed garment
slimmed

sinews laid
sinews laid out in
sinews laid out in stapled cloud
sinews laid out in
sinews laid

Platform

I was seduced by a late-night shadow, and the generative
    reactions of chlorine
and crystal, spreading a fresh plateau.
No amount of scaffold could hold up the colours
which seeped through the gauzy structure at last
as the manual had said they would.
I am not agitated, just a body in dialogue with other bodies
that are not quite bodies, and certainly not our own.
Frameworks contend with weather-bound lethargy.
What is it about the gendering, as you insert more slats in
    the lattice?
It is not as though you meant to grow more fruit on silicone;
I know you men with your steely intentions.
Still, it is sweet with the push and click of something new.
What is it about skin, which is soft in spite of the nails and
    splinters
and secrets long-hammered into wine-mottled doorways?
Wherever the wind blows, our sails shake
and corporations perform a selection of internet speeches
and I grow numb with war. Amoebas of danakil yellow and
    oxide red
bleed symphonic, choke the notes
as though my pores were a chorus. We see them make love
offshore, in celebration of the desert. I am a substance that
    thirsts
for more of whatever you feed it. It is a Thursday by human
    standards
and even these poems are pigments, stinging the peach of
    your fingertips
and their former innocence. We grow silent with the
    chemicals
growing inside us. I wish it would rain forever.

shadow plateau agitated last manual, scaffold slats
   hammered standards
rain sails frameworks shake celebration nails

spreading generative weather-bound lethargy; gendering
meant men intentions yellow red desert chemicals forever
seeped steely speeches sweet amoebas bleed secrets even
   peach feed

crystal pigments stinging fingertips, skin innocence splinters
   click
I I I I I I silent

hold body mottled offshore soft symphonic dialogue
know grow silicone notes grow poems

numb substance love
new human fruit seduced

Gemsong

Nutrient courage
My dearest, the afterlives of us
In plastiglomerate acids, accumulate days.
This too dense to speak. Named
After lindens, lime-shedding silvers
We clasp a genre.
We party
Like it's not the year
It was. Fantasies
Of rain
Macerate lilac pills
And set the Pacific
To gelatine.
A shimmy
Between
These lines.
We fall
Apart like
Teases of silk
Appetitive
Politics
Like glass
Without
The final
Ess.

Nutrient courage afterlives us
plastiglomerate accumulate dense
After shedding genre
We party Like
It was rain
Macerate set
gelatine
lines
fall
silk Appetitive
glass
Without

Fret

stonework at galloping pace	incalculabe flank, bottled	of the hillside	ancient
cutaneous	cutaway	(imperial measures	"convaying sweet water
to euery house/	skin dewy	conduit forgetting	fleshwater
flashflood	stormeye	daisies edged	out of rootstock
falling	tallying	aqueduct's eye-rhyme	capital's rill
slips	at the most wettest part	navigable rural	cycles of drought/
on the face of things	mammal heads networked	small physiological canals	a promising
water feature	draining down	bodies building	drains built
the civitas	glimmering a molecule	carrying the surface	tension breaks
on a whim sweet, twigged drop	ergot	they all fall	down

cutaneous

skin dewy

eye-
rhyme

slips

at the wettest

the civitas

glimmering
ergot

Algal Matters

Bio-architectonic in vault to bloom
A cautious potential; you mentioned Deleuze
Within that immersion, opacity catches us
Backwards, so much green is failing
The ambient impulse to speak.

I was the catalyst of epiphany
Between meat; most often the work does not
Inter-alia with tool and song, the lens of
Tripletting instinct, inset notification
Additive facebook, free of relation

A woman takes off her future shoes
In corporeal modes of infinite pdf, the blues
Of scrolling gesture. Who are we
In the nest again. Ctrl + F
For seed cathedral, shedding

A polymer mood, cells of good
Recalcitrance sealed. A psytrance
Version of slenderness is, a sleep
Can't dance or still. We insulate lightly the non-
Arable alternate. Build in breath.

opacity catches us

Between meat:

Ctrl + F
seed cathedral,

sealed.

Hydrogalvanic

a cycle of nerves. a siting submerged
in the current state of searching for patience,
otherwise patents of the cellular type.

care as unmet precondition for the alkaline
body in refracted light bodied of water,
buoyed between countries, clashing

currency and hearts. electrified sounding
stone, net of inventions a tent in the motions
of wavework takes a generation outliving

itself as domestic collapse. pay fountains
down, stagnates at flash of a bulb: animal,
detector, electrolyte. in the town across

the water, the women sit plenteously
given to flow, circuitous motion a spark
in the channel, which parts and parts.

first leg of experiment—kickback, cathodic—
corrosion is steady, directive, intact.
the trajectory of the dammed is a man-

camp evaporating the porous, breaking
out static and sweat for inflammatory, cut-
and-dried conduit powering up lines and lines.

a
cycle
of
nerves
a
siting
submerged
in
the
current
state
of
searching
for
patience
otherwise
patents
of
the
cellular
type
care
as
unmet
precondition
for
the
alkaline

body
in
refracted
light
bodied
of
water
buoyed
between
countries
clashing
currency
and
hearts
electrified
sounding
stone
net
of
inventions
a
tent
in
the
motions
of
wavework
takes

a
generation
outliving
itself
as
domestic
collapse
pay
fountains
down
stagnates
at
flash
of
a
bulb
animal
detector
electrolyte
in
the
town
across
the
water
the
women
sit

plenteously
given
to
flow
circuitous
motion
a
spark
in
the
channel
which
parts
and
parts
first
leg
of
experiment
kickback
cathodic
corrosion
is
steady
directive
intact
the
trajectory

of
the
dammed
is
a
man
camp
evaporating
the
porous
breaking
out
static
and
sweat
for
inflammat-
ory
cut
and
dried
conduit
powering
up
lines
and
lines

Torrent

The world as waterway, the waterway worlding
the whirl of world. Currencies slur their coins to surrender
and so we exist, and so we attend the rings
of road, the attendant sleep, the music
of not knowing the way you are going. The where.
This air is pure expenditure, we bottled the woodsmoke
for petro-nostalgia. To say you are here
as it says on the sign. Blue as the water
bruises our bodies; every industrial hour and snap
as good as pink and green. We broke it down
and ate all but water. The beats of the light
were ever binaural, then balearic, the way
of a wedding disco depleted. Marriage of anthropos
back into species, becoming again quadruple news.
Mulch is a form and defined withdrawal.
The way we look into pools, the way we
look altogether. The way we look
at ourselves in the water.
I did laps for silence
and did not ask anything of the light.
My gills expensive; my chrysalis
resistant, electric. My breath
the oil on song.

The world as waterway, the waterway worlding
Blue as the water
and ate all but water
ourselves in the water.

Hydrophilic

there was promise in my cells living ghostly metallic
reactively died before I was born. a revolution in picture elements,
smaller and more parts the world wanted to be. or,
hockey sticks in different primary colours, sharply rising
breaths of progressive obsolescence caught in polythene bags,
glow of orange and purple from the carrots inside.
shelves green, I peel a skin every morning, leave to atmospheres,
line your coffers with free sugars, sing a hypermarket strain.
would you believe me if I told this I is real and fertilising.
I choose the most fulsome oranges, practise epiphany
on a friday afternoon: gold leaves, raked soil,
sublime traffic swimming round. I forgot about the island
again: huge tyres you could float on, masses of asphalt,
every prokaryotic child's poisoned skin. beginnings and endings
are always in water, said some fake news I fished out
from a spasming device not made to weather
the measure of life; or, what's undrinkable anyway.
high on smog, baby underneath the cuticles we're all electric blue,
chorus order planetary chromatics from the catalogue gone digital
natives in the fruit aisles, just prepping halloween.
handheld, spectral elements dash across the sonograph,
submerged in exhaust, seismic biceps proteined up.
gilled and gilded we swum brighter, faster than molecules,
which is stretching, really. glittering dissolves overpass;
surface used to be beneath us until milked out and humming.

sugars poisoned digital sharply electric the tyres said wanted
promise life water halloween again skin than about
undrinkable choose I and with breaths is float humming
elements from exhaust brighter biceps hydrophilic and
beginnings afternoon surface caught polythene before soil
dash colours smaller would not I really revolution round
anyway planetary all be me some to epiphany island up
faster the raked huge leave a in you in forgot weather
born across traffic you hypermarket bags be fished every
sticks real living of I orange beneath out a sublime we
and blue the natives or on handheld glittering primary
oranges line the is free out the told the we're aisles leaves
what's peel in order on from to prepping to atmospheres
was catalogue proteined from overpass and a or metallic I
ghostly believe the practise prokaryotic picture swimming I
stretching which rising sonograph your the in this of died
used reactively underneath glow child's to smog spasming
most gilded gilled hockey strain molecules of a always
friday coffers parts milked chromatics high obsolescence
in cells until cuticles endings shelves baby carrots fruit of
I on elements and fertilising masses my asphalt green skin
I submerged news gone gold spectral fulsome dissolves
more world seismic there swum a inside us sing made if
could was the morning different purple progressive device
just in and in every are measure fake chorus

C

Reflecting longest warning, we waited
In seeming, watching the sea
For its lapse of outside, low quality
More than weather is warming
Within annual average
The span of our plateaus
Mediates confidence, the emissions persist
Core of concept, breakable climate
To estimate collapse, try century
The word for plane is pollution, a sort of
Unified vowel we like
Recording precarious animalia
On longer timescales, a case of acidification
& incessant weather, with all accuracy's
Awful eye in lieu of storm
Planting the arrow in limited patches
To clear a little space for timescale
Try being a byproduct
We stood on the farm and watched the pylons
Glower in the wind
& what comes next, a cumulative
Net effect, reaching some nitrous zero
All the children smell like data
They have been frosting their skin with aerosols
For so long their bodies are runways
Of blue plumes showing response to extinction
Is it a simple estimate, the fear in me
Tasting these opiate futures
We waited, watching the vertical axis without panic
A provisionary impact was all we wanted
Counting the irreversible loss
In every obscurity of temperature, halos
Of scarred flesh matching the ozone
In myriad tattoo, tiny islands of epidermal damage

Make of the day a break, another archipelago
The terrestrial risk to seethe in reason
We come without warning, the wires inside us
Sea level rise is only etcetera
And is without limit
To love the perfume of obscurity
In boreal forest, the bleeding spores degrade
Without latitude, a lunar spine collapses
Mycelial dreams of the twentieth century
Is this just lethargy, the glass of the greenhouse
All of this oil just leaking
All of the reefs in the dark seas weeping
All of the venues needing room
At 70% the decline is a gold plaque studded to dusk
In nod to another Byronic sunset
Our populations slide out of livelihood
You say a heat-related morbidity, I say grace
At the table of painkillers
Prodding your sparkling tomatoes for carbon
I am ever so hungry in red
If we wait, undetectable
We cannot adapt to fluvial excess
Wherever we warm in the violet waters, staining
Our sleep with wine-dark oxides
To be carried by night, to wait in the car
Which never was a car, which fell by the moon
With all of our thick, artificial laughter
Who else is laughing, after all?
My little methane, to ask for proportion
Saving the earth as errand, scratch the soil
We remain among cool policy
The order of light is socioeconomic, to say little
Of the rainbow tar, the quartile range of endanger
We cry highly financial tears
Our transitions depleted, crops of the heart
Still wrapped in plastic
Save a little energy for the end now
Intensified diets are all the rain
To mitigate, literature practices absence
Are you in line as we are

Refusing to bloom, click chemistry
So variant, reacting, the sky as tetrazine
Are we 3-4 times higher and lost at sea
As sea is awe, you see in our stranded assets
Locked contingents, our sweet resilience
Never was total
I write the anthropogenic letter, I write it
Slick in the sand
With my tongue of aspartame bubbling
To cover our budget, we ate all the risk
The word for world was never habit
At the gas station, with starbars and coffee
Gauging the air's dispensaries
To wait for natural traffic, in its terrible largesse
The innovation policy clots in all of us
Doesn't even cover the budget.

e	fear	panic	lethargy	crops of the heart / Still wrapped in plastic
miss	hungry	laughing	cry	To love the perfume of obscurity
ions	refusing	resilience	weeping	Wherever we warm in the violet waters

"Beyond"

<through stream through traffic streaming blue-edged
billions of hours of sun. sky-rhyme, superhighway,
tidal brightness microfibred: bodies turning outward
crossing just (some) "enjoying the view". at least
the day gave. back when, leaves open; waiting bodies
close in hundreds times hundreds after, bodies open
photosynthetic flags green against tarmac against
scattered photonswaves. stopped infinitude, blip
in the egg-time amniotic innovation, lignin, suberin density
underwater tissues lagging of decay. skin bare on asphalt,
whose fault, flywheel-powered, stopped the longest
cast iron span. spent carbon alerting. spent carbon
sinking granite piers. spent carbon equipping bicycles,
feet off pedals on oyster blue.
[=bolosaurid, first bipedal, died out in three of six.
amphibian avian reptilian piscine mammalian
invertebrate governance, hexed] from bridges,
streaming towards palatial indecision, rising salt levels de-
crease sedimentary slump. mass on masses rich-limed
lithic coral algal fecal shell debris. cheaper northern, rock
transported over water, gathered steam. there's safety
in <passport> numbers, weather tactics, bugbears photo-
receptive to border software burning somewhere trees.
latecomer passage outwith toll, cite lungs.
close bodies open stream.</>

<through stream   streaming   blue-edged
billions of hours   superhigh
tidal brightness   bodies
crossing   at least
               back when,   waiting bodies
               in hundreds   open
               against tarmac
               infinitude   in the egg-time
amniotic   lignin   asphalt
whose fault   the longest
               spent carbon
                                 oyster blue
bipedal, died   in three of six
               streaming   palatial indecision
mass on masses   limed lithic
                              gathered   safety
in <passport>   weather tactics
                              burning   trees
                                               cite lungs
close bodies   open stream   </>

Acknowledgements

Note on collaboration: we wrote these poems back and forth over the course of a year after spending some time in Orkney in September 2018 for the ASLE-UKI conference, 'A Place on the Edge?' We gave each other prompts, then took it in turns to respond to the poems that emerged through various strategies of breaking, reassembling and drawing energy.

Thank you to Fred, Holly, Laura and Dave for the conversations that started the whirring, and to Evie for the wind and the blue.

LAY OUT YOUR UNREST

www.ingramcontent.com/pod-product-compliance
Lightning Source LLC
Chambersburg PA
CBHW050954030426
42339CB00007B/389